HOW IT'S MADE

Pencils

RUTH THOMSON

PHOTOGRAPHY BY CHRIS FAIRCLOUGH

WATTS BOOKS

LONDON • NEW YORK • SYDNEY

© 1993 Watts Books

Watts Books
96 Leonard Street
London
EC2A 4RH

Franklin Watts Australia
14 Mars Road
Lane Cove
NSW 2066

UK ISBN: 0 7496 1349 1

10 9 8 7 6 5 4 3 2 1

Dewey Decimal Classification: 674
A CIP catalogue record for this book is
available from the British Library

Printed in Malaysia

Contents

Look closely at a pencil

Have you ever had a close look at your coloured pencils?

Coloured pencils are a bit
of a mystery.
Guess the answers
to the questions below.
Then read on to see
if you were right.

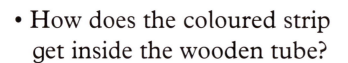

• How does the coloured strip
  get inside the wooden tube?

• What is the coloured strip made from?

• How are pencils painted?

4

What are pencils made of?

Pencils are made of wood, clay, pigment, gum, wax and paint.

The outside of a pencil is made
from a slat of cedar wood.

The coloured strip is made from clay.
A pigment is mixed with the clay
to give it colour.
Gum is added to bind
the mixture together.

The mixture is soaked in wax,
to make it smooth enough
for writing or drawing.

6

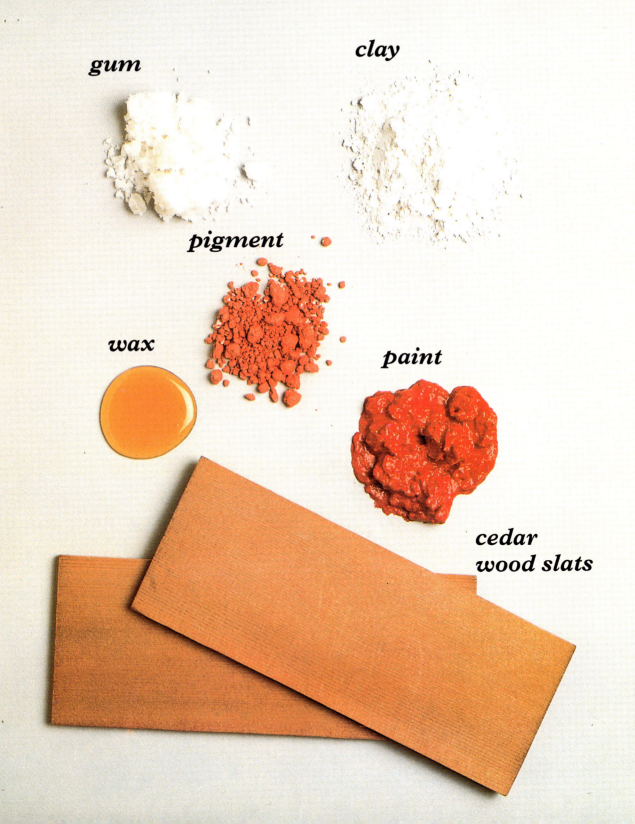

gum

clay

pigment

wax

paint

cedar
wood slats

Weighing and mixing

The ingredients for the coloured strip are mixed together.

The clay and pigment for each colour
are carefully weighed.
They are poured into a giant mixer.
Water and gum are added.

Big mixer hooks stir the mixture.
It looks like breadcrumbs
when it is ready.

Squashing the mixture

The mixture is squashed into a solid cylinder shape.

The crumbly mixture is put
into a hollow cylinder
with a loose plug at the bottom.
Another plug is put on top of it.

A heavy ram comes up from the floor.
It squashes the mixture
between the two plugs
and pushes it out of the machine.
The mixture is now a hard cylinder,
known as a billet.

Making the strips

The billet is made into strips, all exactly the same length.

The billet is forced through a hole
the size of a pencil strip.
It comes out in one length.

This is fed on to a grooved wheel.
Blades cut the lengths
into short strips.

The strips are soft and bendy.
They are put into mesh containers
and heated in an oven.
The heat dries out the water
and hardens the strips.

Waxing the strips

Wax is added to the strips to soften them and help them write smoothly.

The strips are loaded into cans.
The cans are put into a bath of wax.
Can you see why there are holes
near the base?

After six hours, they are taken out and drained.
The strips have absorbed
as much wax as possible.

The cans are whizzed around
in a machine called a centrifuge.
This spins off any extra wax.

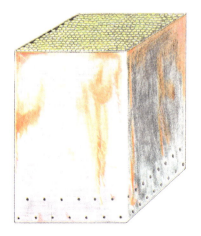

14

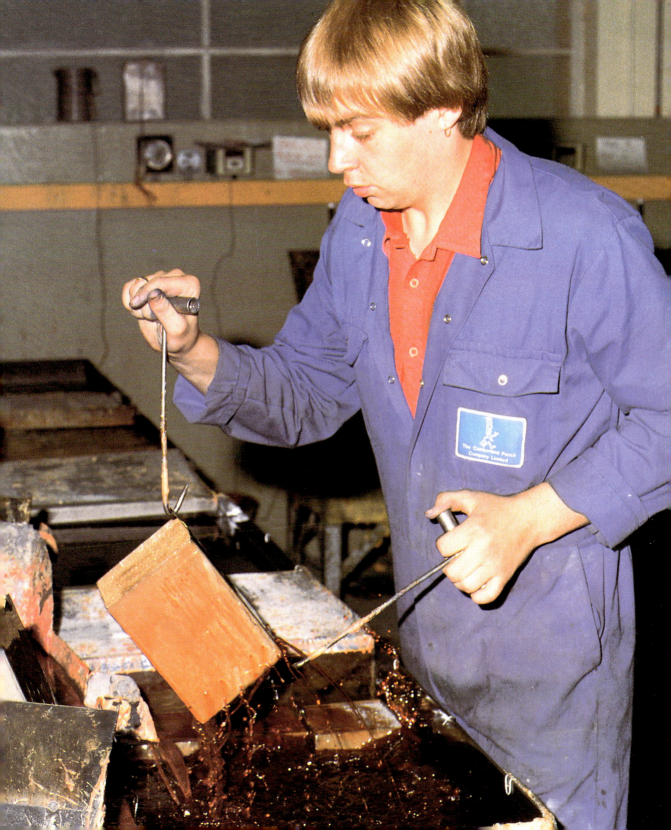

Grooving the wood

A cutter makes grooves in slats of wood for the coloured strips.

A machine loads slats of wood
into the feeder of a cutting machine.
The slats drop on to a conveyor belt.
They pass under a cutter head.

One cutter planes them smooth.
Another notched cutter makes grooves
along the whole length of the slat.
The grooves are semi-circular.

Over half a million slats
can be cut in a day.

16

Fitting the strips

The coloured strips are dropped into the grooves of the slats.

The slats continue travelling
along the conveyor belt.
Nozzles feed glue into each groove.

Some of the slats pass under
a machine which holds the strips.
A turning wheel picks up nine strips
at a time.

It drops them into the grooves
of the slats below.
The glue holds the strips in place.

18

The pencil sandwich

Two slats are joined together to make a pencil sandwich.

A revolving wheel turns the rest
of the slats over.
Each one slides into place
over a slat with strips in,
to make a pencil sandwich.

Several dozen sandwiches are packed
together in a strong clamp.
A press squeezes them tightly
until the glue is hard and dry.

20

Shaping the pencils

The sandwiches are cut into pencils.

A high-speed saw trims the ends of the sandwiches to neaten them.

The sandwiches then pass through shaped cutters.
One set cuts around the top half of the sandwich.

A second set cuts around the bottom half.
The finished pencils drop into an enormous bin.

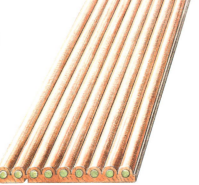

22

Painting the pencils

**The pencils are painted.
The colour matches
the coloured strip inside.**

The plain pencils go through
a bath of paint.
Can you see the rollers
that guide them into it?

They drop on to a conveyor belt.
By the time the pencils reach
the end of it, the paint is dry.
They travel along another conveyor
belt for another coat of paint.
Expensive pencils have
fourteen coats of paint.

Stamping with foil

All pencils are stamped in foil with the name of their maker, range and the country where they were made.

Pencils are stamped using a brass die
with the lettering back to front.
The die is heated and pressed against
some foil on to each pencil in turn.

Run your finger along a pencil
with your eyes shut.
You should easily be able to feel
the dents of the lettering.

26

The finishing touch

The pencils are sharpened to a fine point.

The pencils are stacked in a feeder.
They roll, one by one,
over a moving drum of sandpaper.
As the pencils roll, the points get
sharper and sharper.

Why do you think the metal block
above them has separate 'teeth'?

Packing a set

The pencils are packed in sets ready for you to buy.

The pencils are put in boxes.
Each box contains only one colour.

A packer has all the boxes of colours
for a particular set in front of her.
She always packs the pencils
in the same order.

Would you choose the same order?
Give ten pencils to some friends.
Ask them to put them in their preferred order.
Is their order the same as yours?

Index